LILLENAS®
DRAMA

MOTHER'S & FATHER'S DAY

PROGRAM BUILDER NO. 12

CREATIVE RESOURCES FOR PROGRAM DIRECTORS

COMPILED BY
KIM MESSER

I0806464

lillenas
PUBLISHING COMPANY
PO Box 419527
Kansas City, MO 64141

Questions? Please write or call:

Lillenas Publishing Company
Drama Resources
P. O. Box 419527
Kansas City, MO 64141
Phone: 816-931-1900 • Fax: 816-412-8390
E-mail: drama@lillenas.com
Web Site: www.lillenasdrama.com

Executive Editor: Kim Messer
Supervising Editor: Kimberly Meiste
Manuscript Formatting: Karen Phillips
Cover Design by Brandon Hill
Interior Design by Sharon Page

CONTENTS

Recitations for Preschool 5

Recitations for Ages 5 to 7 7

Recitations for Ages 8 to 10 11

Recitations for Youth and Adults 12

Monologues and Sketches 13

- Mountains Around Me 13
- Supermom 15
- To Be a Dad 20
- Thought for the Day 25
- A Mother's Grief 28

RECITATIONS FOR PRESCHOOL

No One Else

(For a girl)

I love to be with Daddy.
He's strong and funny too.
He makes me laugh and helps me
Like no one else can do.

Evelyn Mika

Thank You, God

(Young children can use sign language in this Hand Action Rhyme)

Thank you, Mom, for your love.
(Thanks sign [full hand out from mouth] to mom)
Thank you, Dad, for your care.
(Thanks sign to dad)
Thank You, God, for giving me
(Thanks sign toward heaven)
These awesome parents I can share. *(Thanks sign toward parents)*

Iris Gray Dowling

Encouragement

A dad or grandpa
Passes the test
If he encourages us
To be our *best*!

Dorothy Heibel

Hi, Dad (Mom)!

I'd be real sad
If I couldn't say,
"Happy Father's (Mother's) Day!"

Dorothy Heibel

My Dad Is Wise

There is no dad like mine *(points to self)*
Who knows just what to say,
And when he doesn't know the answer,
He takes the time to pray.
(Fold hands in prayer)

Iris Gray Dowling

He's My Friend

(For a girl)

I love Daddy and he loves me.
We play horsie on his knee.
We practice counting—one, two, three.
He's my friend . . . *and* fam-i-ly.

Evelyn Mika

Our Prayer

For our dear dad (mom)
We say a prayer
With a *Thank You* for
Always being there.

Dorothy Heibel

A Good Friend

What a *great friend*
A dad (mom) can be . . .
A *blessing* from God
To you and me!

Dorothy Heibel

Father's Day

Father's Day can be
A great day from the start
When we show our Father
The love that's in our heart.

Dorothy Heibel

It's Mommy!

I know somebody who loves me.
I know somebody who cares.
I know somebody who's always there.
I know somebody—it's Mommy!

Mommy's somebody who loves me.
Mommy's somebody who cares.
Mommy's somebody who's always there.
I know somebody—it's Mommy!

L. Ruth Carter

A Mother Teaches

The mother eagle with chicks in the nest
Shows them all what she does best.
She stretches her wings and soars to the sky
And teaches them to jump up and fly.

The mother pony with a colt at her side
Shows him what is a horse's pride.
She kicks up her heels and gallops in fun
And teaches him to leap out and run.

The mother dolphin with a calf in the sea
Shows her child what brings her glee.
She dives down deep, then returns with a grin
And teaches him to plunge in and swim.

My mother teaches me what she does best
And because of that, I'm very blessed,
For she teaches me about God above
And by her example, how to love.

L. Ruth Carter

RECITATIONS FOR AGES 5 TO 7

My Father Loves Me

(May be given by either a boy or girl, and may be replaced with "Mother.")

I know my father loves me,
It's very plain to see
The way he prays, and cares for,
And watches over me.

Evelyn Mika

Parents

Parents are great
When our spirits they lift.
They truly are a
God-given gift!

Dorothy Heibel

Just like You

(For 2 boys)

Boy 1: You fix the car and wash the dog
And build a tree house too.
I hope when I grow up
That I'll be just like you.
Boy 2: You say your prayers and go to church,
Take care of Mommy, too.
I know when I grow up
That I'll be just like you!

Evelyn Mika

A Special Dad (Mom)

Jesus loves me everyday.
This I know is true.
He cares for me and guides me
Through a special dad (mom) like you.

Evelyn Mika

Fathers Are Special

(For 6 children, each Child holding up their letter to spell "Father")

All: My father is special; he does so many things,
Child 1 (F): Fixes my broken toys.
Child 2 (A): Advises me well.
Child 3 (T): Takes out the trash.
Child 4 (H): Helps with my homework.
Child 5 (E): Enjoys spending time with our family.
Child 6 (R): Rakes the leaves in our yard.
All: Thank you, Father, for everything you do!

Wanda E. Brunstetter

Dads

A dad's a combination
Of strength and love,
And God's special help
From above.

Dorothy Heibel

The Heavenly Kind

(For a girl)

My father works so hard each day
But doesn't seem to mind.
He loves, provides, and cares for
me.
He's the heavenly kind.

Evelyn Mika

Daddy's Home

(For a boy)

"Daddy's home," I shout it out,
The two best words each day,
Cause that's when supper's ready,
Then, we go out and play.

Dad throws the ball; we take a
walk
Or wrestle on the floor.
When the fun is done, can't wait,
again,
'Til Daddy's at the door!

Evelyn Mika

To Mom

Mom, you make home
Such a likable place.
Home wouldn't be home
Without your loving face!
Happy Mother's Day!

Dorothy Heibel

My Dad

I'll tell you about a wonderful
man—
It's my dad who's the greatest
one.
He knows when to take me to
church,
And to school, and to places
of fun.

Iris Gray Dowling

When I'm a Mother

When I'm a mother I want to be
As loving as my mother is to me.
When I'm a mother I'll show my
love,
Like God does from His home
above.

Wanda E. Brunstetter

Thanks for Dads

Though each dad is different
And does his own thing,
We're thankful for them
And their praises we sing!

Dorothy Heibel

Show Me, Daddy

(For a girl)

I can't see God,
    But He sees me.
So, show me, Daddy,
    What my eyes can't see.

Do His bidding
    And do your part
To make Him real
    Within my heart.

Evelyn Mika

Mothers Are Special

(For 6 children, each Child *holding up a letter to spell out "Mother")*

All: My mother is special; she does so many things,

Child 1 (M): Makes the beds and cleans the house.

Child 2 (O): Obeys God's Word.

Child 3 (T): Teaches me how to pray.

Child 4 (H): Holds my hand when I'm afraid.

Child 5 (E): Eagerly teaches me about God.

Child 6 (R): Reads me Bible stories.

All: Thank you, Mother, for everything you do!

Wanda E. Brunstetter

Dad

A helpful, friendly
    Guy is Dad,
One of the best friends
    I've ever had!

Dorothy Heibel

My Daddy Cares

I might be just a little kid
    But I know a thing or two.
I know my daddy cares for me,
    I know it, 'cause it's true!

When I'm sad he reaches me
    And wipes my tears away.
When I'm bad he teaches me
    To listen and obey.

When I'm mad he brings to me
    Comfort in my fears.
When I'm glad he sings with me
    And laughs and smiles and cheers.

I might be just a little kid
    But I know a thing or two.
I know my Daddy cares for me,
    I know it, 'cause it's true!

L. Ruth Carter

Jesus' Mother

Mary was Jesus' mother,
She loved Him, oh so much.
She nurtured Him and guided Him,
With wisdom and a gentle touch.

Mary was the kind of woman
God wants all mothers to be.
She believed in her Son and followed Him
All the way to Calvary's Tree.

Wanda E. Brunstetter

It's True

Dads come in all sizes
Short, medium, and tall.
Each is original
For God made them all!

Dorothy Heibel

What Does My Daddy Do?

What does my daddy do?
What does he do for me?

He smiles, he cries, he works, he plays,
He shows me how to share.
He reads, he drives, he laughs, he prays,
He shows me how to care.

What does my daddy do?
That's what he does for me!

L. Ruth Carter

RECITATIONS FOR AGES 8 TO 10

Your Way

(For boy or girl)

Father, God, I thank You
For loving me each day
Through the dad (mom) You've given me—
My life, Your will . . . Your way!

Evelyn Mika

To Honor You

(For boy or girl)

We're here today to honor you
For all the many things you do.
Thank you, Dad (Mom), for your great love,
Reflecting Father God's above.

Evelyn Mika

You Take Care of Me

(For boy or girl)

I know my heavenly Father,
He isn't hard to see
Because you show His tender love
As you take care of me.

Evelyn Mika

On Father's Day

A dad provides good company
And plays an important role in the family.
So, Dad, on your special day of days
May you be blessed in many ways.

Dorothy Heibel

Thank You, Dad

(For a boy)

Thank you, Dad, for all you do.
Thanks for who you are.
Thanks for your love and patience
That's grown me up this far.

Evelyn Mika

God's Great Call

(For a boy)

My dad's the greatest in the world.
He outshines them all
By helping, teaching, loving me.
He's answered God's great call.

Evelyn Mika

RECITATIONS FOR YOUTH AND ADULTS

You Are My Hero

(A reading for a teen boy or adult male)

Dad, you are my hero,
Even though, right from the start
You gave to me the starring role,
Yourself, the lesser part.

I realize the strength now
It took to walk away
Instead of criticizing
My foolishness that day.

Your patience and your fortitude
Have undergirded me,
Created wings of steel to fly
Just where I need to be.

You've demonstrated on your knees
How big a man you are,
By praying for your family
Which you have brought so far.

You've shown me how to live a life
That's strong, and real, and true,
A way that leads—yet follows,
    Dad,
. . . Just by being you!

Evelyn Mika

Happy Father's Day!

Dads may take kids fishing
    Or to a baseball game.
Of course, dads are all different,
    They don't do things the same.
But when they show their families
    The awesome gift of love,
We know why God made dads
And say,
    "Many thanks to the Lord
        above!"

Dorothy Heibel

MONOLOGUES AND SKETCHES

Mountains Around Me

by Pauline J. Sheehan

Running Time: 6 minutes

Themes: Honoring fathers, Family

Cast:

Son or Daughter

Son/Daughter: From my canvas chair, I scan the mountains around me. Although my thoughts ricochet from mountain to mountain, I feel nestled between them. They remind me of looking across the Kidron chasm to the Mount of Olives. "As the mountains are round about Jerusalem, so the Lord is round about his people."

I scan the southern horizon where I remember Daddy trudging with us over dusty trails and climbing up steep, treacherous cliffs, clamoring over boulders and scooting into canyons. We collect Owyhee Picture Rock, Petrified Wood, and Thunder Eggs. Then we hang around Daddy's shed, which overflows with rock saws, tumblers, polishing wheels, display cases, and jewelry. Proudly, Daddy adorns his daughters with rock necklaces, earrings, and bracelets, and his sons with belt buckles and rope ties.

To the northeast, the Blue Mountains jag sharply to the Rockies. The river snakes between Oregon and Idaho, then burrows into Hell's Canyon.

The mountains to the north remind me of family camp-outs: frying fish, swatting mosquitoes, and dodging campfire smoke. Memories of pine cones and purple sunsets, butterflies and bluebirds, falling tents and wet socks linger in my heart.

From the high western plains, the Owyhee reservoir harnesses the floods, then releases the water to irrigate this Treasure Valley Desert. Loose, fertile soil absorbs heat from the sun and miraculously produces crops like sugar beets, onions, alfalfa, wheat, and what Daddy grows—apples and potatoes and corn.

From the east, myriad shades of luminescent light burst below fluffy clouds, bathing the horizon in a warm glow, while rays of sunrise rapture upward. Breath-taking abundance fills the sky with its unlimited beauty. "Look, God made me an Easter card . . . a heaven-sized, real-life, resurrection painting."

"God, who is rich in mercy." The phrase catches my ear, reminding me that I am at an outdoor service. I glance at the lithe pastor standing near me. His cowboy boots dig into the grass. No horse, ho hat, no guitar. Mercy is a small, but heavy word. But it is a familiar word in our home because Daddy is totally in awe that such a great God loves our family.

As a farmer, Daddy knows that his crops are at God's mercy. Hopefully, spring frosts won't freeze the apple blossoms, the summer hail storms won't peck the apples, yet the Indian Summer sun will blush them to ripeness. Daddy can't depend upon the weather, but he teaches us to depend upon God, who is rich in mercy.

I hear another phrase, "by grace are you saved." Grace seems like a theological word, but I know what it means. How do I know? Because of Daddy. Day after day, as we irrigate corn, and pick apples, and explore the mountains, Daddy is always there. He is compassionate and loving, not because we deserve it, but because we are his children.

"Not of works." The pastor holds a large Bible. Its blue tattered cover is taped with electric tape. I know this pastor uses his Bible until it is well-worn, but . . . I accept him for his character: modest, obedient, servant-like, more concerned with the contents than the cover.

He continues, "I am reading the words from Joe's Bible. He has penciled in the margins by Ephesians chapters two and three."

Jolted to the immediate surroundings, I recognize that the pastor is reading from Daddy's large print Gideon Bible. Glancing around, I see Mom sitting rigidly, children clasping roses, and flowers brushing my knees. My brother's harmonica wafts *Rock of Ages* as the pastor concludes. "Ye, being rooted and grounded in love, may be able to comprehend . . . the breadth and length and depth and height; and to know the love of Christ . . ."

I know that God's love is whopping and enormous, wide and vast, colossal and tremendous. Why do I know that? Because even though Daddy has labored through eighty-five harvest seasons, his ministry is not over. His influence goes on demonstrating the awesomeness of Christ's love.

Neighbors and family and friends mill around. They have experienced God's grace as Daddy's unassuming kindness. Some of them say that Daddy fed their cows when they were sick, some say that he visited them in prison, some say he invited them to breakfast, and some say he was honest in all of his dealings. Some reject his God, some eat apples from his orchard, some read the Gideon Bibles he gave them, some admire the Oregon Trail mural on his house, and some carry his heart-shaped rocks in their pockets. Some say that he loved his wife and family. Everyone says, "Joe was a man who loved God."

Here I am, sitting on this canvas sling chair, which is waiting for an excuse to dump me. Yet, I am comforted that mountains are round about me, Daddy's heritage nurtures me, and God's arms hug me.

Supermom

by Lin Sexton

Running Time: 6 minutes

Themes: Motherhood, Parenting, Overachieving parents

Scripture Reference: Ephesians 6:1-4

Suggested Use: Youth and Adult audiences

Synopsis: Sitting in a doctor's waiting room, three young pregnant women discuss parenting. When it's discovered that one woman's children are overachieving geniuses, the other two ladies respond—one with shock and self doubt, and one with a sweet, sensible calm. Along the way, we can't help but laugh!

Cast:

Jo Beth—A sweet country girl, earthy and southern; in her 20s

Gale—Early 30s; a Harvard grad raising a large family of geniuses; always calm, she intimidates the others without meaning to

Cathy—A high-strung woman in her first pregnancy; easily worried and reactionary

Props:

3 or more waiting room chairs

Coffee table with magazines
3 purses or tote bags

Costumes: All the women should wear maternity clothes and appear to be in various stages of pregnancy

Production Note: Keep tone sitcom style

(Sitting in a waiting room, two pregnant women are thumbing through magazines, waiting for their doctor's appointments. A third enters and stands for a bit, clearly exhausted and hot. There are no children onstage; yet they are watched and spoken to as if they are in the room. Jo Beth *is an earthy, country girl with a southern accent.* Cathy *is an emotional, high-strung "everywoman."* Gale *is the perfect and brilliant clichéd supermom who has answers for every question in life.)*

Jo Beth *(fanning herself):* Sure is hot in this office. Whewee. Mercy.

Cathy: Are you OK? You better sit down.

Jo Beth: Thanks, darlin.

Cathy: Are you . . . due pretty soon?

Jo Beth *(friendly smile):* You know, I am just not real sure. This is my first appointment and I'm hopin' to find out that very thing.

(Amazed, Gale *and* Cathy *do a take as* Jo Beth *sits down slowly. Next lines spoken to unseen—except by actresses—children located off to one side in an imaginary play area.)*

Gale *(looking to children):* Christopher! Sit down and read a magazine.

Cathy *(astounded):* He can read? That little guy?

Gale *(matter-of-fact):* Oh sure.

Cathy: Uh . . . how old is he—the one with the magazine?

Gale: Three.

Cathy *(to herself):* I was afraid of that.

Jo Beth: Mercy me, those are smart children.

Gale *(almost clinical in her tone and approach):* Kelly, Mommy told you to tie your shoes.

Cathy: Don't tell me.

Gale: Kelly! Now, please.

Cathy: She's tying her shoes. No way. What is she, about three?

Gale: Yeah. They're twins.

Cathy: Three? I can't believe it. I didn't think kids learned to tie their shoes until . . . they were about in junior high. You must be supermom.

Gale: Me? Hardly. *(For her this is no big deal.)* You should see my triplets. They're going through a stage. All they do is fight.

Cathy *(skeptical):* How old?

Gale: Five.

Cathy *(instantly comparing her own experience and expectations, she is stunned):* All three of them are five?

Jo Beth *(does a take to them this time):* Well, sure.

Gale: Yes.

Cathy *(defensive):* I knew that.

Gale: Christopher! No, no. You let Kelly finish her magazine. *(Beat)* No—you may not have the *Newsweek*! You finish your *US News* first.

Cathy *(giving up):* Let me guess. You have triplets and they do higher math.

Gale: Math? *(Laughs)* Hardly. I have trouble getting them to practice their violin. Their Suzuki teacher is getting frustrated with them.

Jo Beth *(in wonder):* They're learnin' karate?

Cathy: Suzuki.

Jo Beth: They ride motorcycles?

Gale: No. You know, Suzuki.

Jo Beth: Don't tell me you let those kids eat raw fish?

Gale: Of course not.

Cathy *(almost whispers it to her):* It's a kind of music lessons. For kids.

Jo Beth: Why?

Cathy: Let me get this straight. They are doing higher math?

Gale: No, no, no. *(*Cathy *and* Jo Beth *give sighs of relief.)* Charlie and I don't think it's wise to start them on math until we're sure they've gotten a hold of abstract thinking. You know.

Cathy *(slightly sarcastic):* Oh. Yeah. I know what you mean. *(Beat)* How do you tell?

Gale: Tell?

Cathy: You know. How do you tell they've gotten a hold of abstract thinking.

Gale *(smiling innocently):* Oh, you know. Kids kind of just pick it up. Michael, my nine year old just started doing algebraic equations with his Alphabits Cereal one day when he was about five. It was so cute . . . he said, "Look, Mom. There aren't enough X's in my Alphabits." That's when we realized he was getting it.

Jo Beth: How many kids do y'all have?

Gale: Six. I just hope, for their sake, that this one *(patting tummy)* is a solo act.

Cathy: Do you know yet?

Gale: I find out today. It's sonogram time!

Cathy: You've got this motherhood thing really down.

Gale: I just want my kids to have the best life possible. Can't start too early. You have to prepare them for the competition.

Jo Beth *(triumphant—like she finally has connected with what they're talking about):* Well, I believe in Little League.

Gale *(looks at her like she's from Mars):* Uh huh.

Cathy: Really. How do you have kids like that? *(Before* Gale *can answer* Cathy *has gotten so worked up she interrupts.)* I mean, you really must be rich or something. Oh, that's rude. I'm sorry . . . but I have to know. OK. You can tell me. You don't know me so hey—tell me. Is there something wrong with me? I mean, do I look like an OK person? I don't know, motherhood is just kind of pushing me over the edge. Maybe it's hormones. Maybe it's me. I can't do it all. I mean, do you have a nanny? You must. When do you sleep? What do they eat—some kind of special vitamins?

GALE *(wanting to get away from* CATHY*)*: Kelly? Chris? If you two are good you can go in with Mommy and see the sonogram. Would you like that? *(She listens to them.)*

JO BETH *(aside)*: Six to one says they would.

GALE *(talking to her kids)*: Well, I don't know how big the screen is but I'm sure you can see just fine. Of course it's high def. Come on, now, gather up your stuff. I'm going to check on my appointment. You can go over there to the fish tank and see how many varieties of fish you can count. I'll be right back. *(She exits.)*

CATHY: I can't do this. *(Starts to cry—in a hysterical entertaining manner)* I can't do this. I wasn't made to be a mother. I can't even balance my checkbook, much less teach preschoolers the difference between carp and barracuda!

JO BETH: Well, somethin' tells me most preschoolers don't much care.

CATHY: But my baby will grow up deprived. How will it catch up? Look at the competition! I mean, me, I'm scared to death of computers. So that's out. I don't speak any other languages. I'm tone deaf. So the music thing is out. I guess I could try to teach it . . . like maybe a few things like . . .

JO BETH *(fanning again)*: Mercy, it's hot in here.

CATHY: You know . . . "Mary had a little lamb."

JO BETH: Being pregnant is hard enough without puttin' yourself through this.

CATHY: But I can't be a supermom, a mom of the times. So how can I raise my kids and have them turn out? Help them compete? Be winners?

JO BETH *(after a beat, she says in a sweet tone)*: Just love 'em, honey. You just gotta love 'em.

CATHY: What?

JO BETH: My mama had eleven of us . . . one at a time. We couldn't tie our shoes 'cause we didn't have no shoes. But darlin', we sure had fun. And we was happy 'cause we knew Mama'd rather be with us than anybody.

CATHY *(suddenly sober):* And?

JO BETH: And she never tried to be any supermom. She was just our Mama. She loved us and that's all we knew. I don't reckon she compared herself to nobody. I don't reckon she had time.

CATHY: Did you all turn out OK? Oh please tell me you weren't criminals or crazy or—

JO BETH: Well, sure. We turned out. We had our ups and downs. Mama loved us with a good, strong love. She wasn't trying to make us into anybody we weren't.

CATHY: Anybody who raises eleven kids has to have some trade secrets.

JO BETH: Mama didn't have no trade secrets. She just loved us, loved the Lord, and loved our daddy, and that made home a good place to be.

CATHY *(to herself, hopefully):* Just love them. *(Beat)* Just love them. *(Smile)* Yeah. I can do that!

(Blackout)

To Be a Dad

by L. Ruth Carter

Running Time: Approximately 6 minutes

Theme: New fatherhood anxiety

Synopsis: A young pastor is terrified of becoming a dad

Cast:

JASON—Pastor
MAUREEN—Wise, grandmotherly, church secretary

Props:

Stack of papers (membership list)
Telephone
Office desk and chairs

*(*Jason *is kneeling to gather scattered papers from his office floor.)*

Maureen *(entering, stops when she sees* Jason*):* Being on one's knees is undoubtedly good exercise. *(Beat)* But I can think of better things to do once I'm down there.

Jason: Huh?

Maureen: Prayer, Jase, honey. Prayer

Jason *(standing):* Oh. Yeah. I dropped the membership roll.

Maureen *(nods):* I see.

Jason: Yes. Well. *(Stacks papers on desk; they fall again)* Oh, brother! *(Kneels)*

Maureen: Jason. *(*Jason *mutters to himself.)* Jason!

Jason *(blinks):* What?

Maureen: I hope those are prayers you're muttering down there.

Jason: Uh. Yeah. *(Stands, putting papers on desk)*

Maureen *(grabs papers):* Let me do that. *(Examines them)* Good grief! What a mess!

Jason: Uh, yeah.

Maureen: Your conversation is sparkling with wit, today. What are you doing with these papers?

Jason: Looking for Conrad's cell phone number.

Maureen: Why not get it from your computer?

Jason: I wiped it.

Maureen: You wiped it? Conrad's number?

Jason: Yes. No. I mean, yes. Conrad's number. I mean the whole thing.

Maureen: The whole thing? You mean the *entire* membership roll?

Jason: Yeah. That's why I got the hard copy.

Maureen: How'd you do that?

Jason: I was writing my sermon.

MAUREEN: You do that every week without mishap.

JASON: Well, I wiped the sermon. I couldn't get it back. I tried everything. I wanted Conrad's advice. Couldn't find his number.

MAUREEN: Sounds like you've had quite a day.

JASON: Yeah. And it's only 8:30 in the morning. I have to get through at least 14 more hours before I can go to bed.

MAUREEN: I've never seen you like this. You've always had it together, calm, cool, and collected. Even your blue jeans are immaculately pressed!

JASON *(affronted):* They are not!

MAUREEN: And you've never had trouble with the computer before. What gives?

JASON: Just one of those days.

MAUREEN: What's the trouble?

JASON: Oh, you know. This and that.

MAUREEN: Oh, that's real helpful. I'll bet you let your counseling clients get away with that.

JASON: You're not my counselor.

MAUREEN: No, I'm your secretary, which is even better. Spill it!

JASON: Debbie and I are going to have a baby.

MAUREEN *(drops papers):* You what?

JASON: Yeah. *(Both kneel to gather papers)* We're pregnant. *(Gulps)* I'm going to become a father.

MAUREEN: Why, that's wonderful! *(Big hug)* Congratulations! But what's bothering you?

JASON *(pacing):* I'm scared stiff.

MAUREEN: That's understandable. It's a huge commitment. *(Putting the membership roll in order)*

JASON: What if I'm not a good father?

MAUREEN: You won't be a perfect one. No one is. But I'm sure you and Debbie will make fine parents.

JASON: Oh, yes! Debbie'll be great. But me—I just don't know if I have what it takes.

MAUREEN: What does it take?

JASON: What?

MAUREEN: What *does* it take to be a good father?

JASON: I dunno. *(Beat)* Playing catch.

MAUREEN: Did your father play catch with you?

JASON: Yeah, he did.

MAUREEN: Did that make him a good dad?

JASON: I thought so.

MAUREEN: Why?

JASON: It made me feel he liked being with me. That he enjoyed my company *because* I was a kid, not in spite of it.

MAUREEN *(smiles):* Nice.

JASON: Yeah.

MAUREEN: What else?

JASON: He provided for us. *(Grins)* I took that for granted.

MAUREEN: Normal for kids.

JASON: And he's honest. He lost a promotion because of his integrity. Several times. Didn't resent it. Said if he didn't live by his principles, he'd have no principles to live by.

MAUREEN: Quite an example.

JASON: Yeah. Dad was a quiet kind of guy. Yet when we had family devotions, he was strong and true. A spiritual leader. We kids respected that.

MAUREEN: Absolutely essential.

Jason: It sure is. *(Laughs)* You know, I just thought of something. You know what made me feel secure in my little world?

Maureen: What?

Jason: He loved my mom. He cherished her. When I was snotty and mouthed off, he really came down on me. He respected her, allowed her to be herself.

Maureen: And so, you grew up seeing your mother as a person of worth.

Jason *(with new understanding):* Yeah.

Maureen: As you now see Debbie as a person of worth.

Jason: Yeah.

Maureen: But that's not all, is it?

Jason: Not by a long shot. His faith in God was so steady. It colored everything. If he had doubts from time to time, I never saw it. What I did see was a man on his knees.

Maureen: On his knees, eh.

Jason: Yeah.

Maureen: Quite a check list.

Jason *(nods):* I know. *(Touch of panic)* How can I ever measure up?

Maureen: Your dad ever make mistakes?

Jason: Plenty of times. Nobody's perfect.

Maureen: And you won't be either, *(grins)* even if you *are* a minister and you're supposed to be.

Jason: I just don't want to be a schmuck.

Maureen: I'm afraid you will be, sometimes. Whatever a schmuck is. But mostly you'll just be a dad. Follow your father's example, but don't compare yourself to him. Rely on him and your mom for advice. After all, they've already done it once, and didn't do such a bad job!

Jason: Gee, thanks.

MAUREEN: There's one thing you can copy that'll give you an edge that nothing can beat.

JASON: What's that?

MAUREEN *(stands, throws her neatly stacked pile of papers on the floor):* Get on your knees, Jason. The more time you spend there will equip you for the time on your feet better than anything else.

*(*JASON *kneels to gather papers.* MAUREEN *goes to the door as if to exit, pauses for next line.)*

MAUREEN: God bless you, Daddy Jason! *(Exits)*

Thought for the Day

by Lin Sexton

Running Time: 4 minutes

Theme: The things our mothers do for us

Suggested Use: All audiences

Synopsis: Two women banter about the precious, amazing, and often funny things moms do for their families

Cast:

WOMAN 1—30s or 40s
WOMAN 2—30s or 40s

Props:

2 readers theatre folders

Costumes: Contemporary

Production Note: Tone should be comedic but not overdone—let the lines speak for themselves

WOMAN 1: Thought for the day—

WOMAN 2: When you get to the end of the day—

WOMAN 1: the very end—

Woman 2: and you lay your head on your pillow, do you really know which one of the roles you played today is really you?

Both: Hmmm . . .

Woman 1: Of all the hats you wore today, which one did you like the best—

Woman 2: hate the most?

Both *(beat):* Discuss. *(Beat)*

Woman 1: Well, let's see, today I was a cook, florist . . .

Woman 2: Computer repair woman, answering service, cook . . .

Woman 1: Internet policewoman, dishwasher, medic, personal shopper . . .

Woman 2: Cook . . .

Woman 1: Tutor, banker, organizer, interior decorator . . .

Woman 2: Exterminator, cook—

Woman 1: I hope those two don't go together.

Woman 2: You don't want to know.

Woman 1: Videographer, soccer mom, labor negotiator—

Woman 2: I don't care if Billy's mom pays him to mow the lawn. You're do ing it for free.

Woman 1: Cleaning lady, movie reviewer . . .

Woman 2: Movie police . . .

Both: Cook . . .

Woman 1: Travel agent, backseat driver—

Woman 2: Honey! Why don't you just hook on to that guy's bumper and save gas! *(Meekly)* Sorry.

Woman 1: Gift wrapper, homework police—

Woman 2: What do you mean you have to build a project by tomorrow?

Woman 1: Mechanic, fund-raiser—

WOMAN 2: No! They can't do this to me! I am on a diet and the school's having another candy sale!

WOMAN 1: Aerobics drop out, window washer . . .

WOMAN 2: Voter, precinct walker, fireman—

WOMAN 1: Hello, Sally? Can you do my nails again right away? I know you did them yesterday, but I was lighting Susie's birthday candles and my thumbnail caught on fire.

WOMAN 2: Animal trainer, gardener—

WOMAN 1: Did you know weeds grow faster than grass? And they take less water?

WOMAN 2: Hazardous waste removal expert . . .

WOMAN 1: Laundress, economist—

WOMAN 2: Let's see. Where can we get the most fast food for the least money?

WOMAN 1: Child Psychologist, Pseudo Nutritionist—

WOMAN 2: So, if I buy vegetables and put them in the front of the fridge where we can see them, then we'll feel better about what we're really eating.

WOMAN 1: Miracle worker—

WOMAN 2: So, I took your shirts to the cleaners because there were Crayolas in the dryer.

WOMAN 1: Fashion consultant—No, Gloria. That looks good on you. Really.

WOMAN 2: Sister, daughter, in-law . . .

WOMAN 1: Veterinarian—What's that thumping sound, kids? Kids? Hey you guys didn't put the cat in the dryer again, did you?

WOMAN 2: Funeral director—OK, find a shoe box big enough to put the cat in and tell Annie to stop crying.

WOMAN 1: Jog-a-thon mom—That's it. I refuse to let my children take part in *anything* that has the words a-thon in the name.

WOMAN 2: Chauffeur—No. I'm more like the bus driver in *Speed*.

Woman 1: Detective—I found out why the kids were up till eleven last night. There were candy wrappers in their beds.

Woman 2: Story teller, Home Group leader, painter, animal trainer . . .

Woman 1: Rock collector, bug collector, reluctant science fair competitor, shrink, Sunday school teacher, librarian, crisis manager—

Woman 2: So, there I was on the phone, gosh it couldn't have been more than five minutes. And the boys lifted the four railroad ties that formed the sides of the sandbox and they stood them up on end and yelled, "Look Mom, we built a fort!"

Woman 1: That's enough for one day. Don't you think?

Woman 2: Sure. It starts all over again tomorrow.

Woman 1: You know, I think the phrase "working women" is redundant.

(Blackout)

A Mother's Grief

by Gordon Williams

Running Time: Approximately 9 minutes

Theme: The cost of motherhood

Scripture References: Matthew 20:20-28; Mark 10:35-45; John 19, 25-27; Acts 12:1-5

Synopsis: 44 A.D. James, brother of John, son of Salome, has just been beheaded by order of Herod Agrippa I, King of Judea. James is the first of the Twelve Apostles to be martyred. Salome, James' mother, is in mourning for him as her other son John, along with Mary, mother of the Messiah, comes to offer comfort.

Cast:

Salome—Mother of James and John, the "Sons of Thunder"
Mary—Mother of Jesus Christ
John—Son of Salome, adopted son of Mary, apostle of Jesus

*(*Salome, *clad in mourning clothes, sits CS. Her son* John, *with her sister* Mary, *mother of Jesus, enter from SL.)*

MARY: Oh, Salome.

SALOME *(rising):* Mary . . . Mary . . . oh, my sister! *(Rushes to* MARY. *They embrace, then she turns to* JOHN.*)* Oh, John, my son . . . my son, my son! *(They embrace.)*

JOHN: We came as soon as we heard.

SALOME: You must forgive me for being such a poor hostess.

MARY: No, Salome, you mustn't upbraid yourself. I know how you must feel this moment. You were with me at Golgotha. Surely you remember what I was going through.

SALOME: Golgotha . . . I was there with you, and the Magdalene. Yes, I was there.

JOHN: I was there also, Mother.

SALOME: Yes, my son. I know. It all comes back to me now.

MARY: Now, it's my turn to be here for you.

SALOME: You're so kind, Mary. So very kind . . . *(Sits again)* You must excuse me while I regain my composure.

MARY: We understand, Salome. Take your time. All the time you need.

SALOME: At least James' death was quicker. They tell me beheading is usually reserved for Roman citizens. You had to see your Son suffer on that hideous cross!

MARY: But Jesus' death was much quicker than most of those who are crucified. We must thank His Father for that.

SALOME: . . . His Father . . .

JOHN: Our Father.

SALOME: Yes, *our* Father.

JOHN: Did you hear that James actually converted his executioner?

SALOME: He did?

JOHN: He gave his testimony to the executioner, right there before King Agrippa, his court, and everyone else who was present in the arena. The executioner then threw down his sword and accepted Jesus as his Savior. So Agrippa had to call in someone else to take up that sword and cut off both their heads!

SALOME: James did that?

JOHN: Yes, Mother. Some of those who witnessed it are right there in the next room.

MARY: You must be so proud.

SALOME *(rising from her chair):* Do you remember, John, that time when I went to Jesus and boldly demanded that He decide which one of you boys was to sit on His right and the other to sit on His left?

JOHN: I'll never forget it!

SALOME: "It is not for me to decide that," He said to me, sternly. "That is for My Father to determine."

JOHN: The other apostles were furious with us.

SALOME: And I felt like such a fool!

JOHN: But then Jesus rebuked us all, telling us we were acting no better than the Gentiles. "Whoever wants to be great among you must be willing to become your servant . . . for the Son of Man came not to be served but to serve." *(Pause)* Then he added, "and to give His life a ransom for many."

SALOME: And that He did at Golgotha.

MARY: There was no other way.

JOHN: That's what He kept trying to tell us when He was here on this earth.

SALOME: . . . no other way.

JOHN: He also warned us there would be danger; that we could be killed too. First Stephen, now James.

SALOME: That doesn't make it any easier to bear.

MARY *(taking* SALOME's *hand):* I know.

JOHN: We can take comfort in knowing both Stephen and James are now in heaven with Jesus. And Peter may follow.

Salome: Peter . . . ?

John: He's just been arrested, Mother. He's under heavy guard.

Salome: Oh, no, not Peter!

John: Word is, Agrippa's planning to have him killed right after Passover.

Salome: We must pray for him, then.

Mary: He's already being prayed for in the next room.

Salome: Peter's wife—is she out there?

Mary: Yes, I spoke with her.

Salome *(rising):* I must go to her, also.

John: In time, Mother. Right now, I think you ought to rest.

Mary: I think so too. You're going through so much now.

Salome *(sitting again):* I haven't thought to ask how either of you are doing all this time.

Mary: We're fine, Salome. We're doing just fine.

John: We've been very busy. There's so much work to do.

Mary: There's been so much work for all of us.

Salome: Yes, so much work . . . *(Pause)* It doesn't seem that long ago, does it?

John: What do you mean, Mother?

Salome: When we all stood before that cross, and Jesus looked down on you, Mary, saying, in that pain-filled voice, "Woman, behold your son!"

Mary: I remember it very well, Salome.

Salome: Then He turned His head toward you, John, and declared, "Behold your mother!"

John: Yes, Mother, I remember.

Mary: How did you feel, Salome?

Salome: I didn't know what to think, at first. It was all very surprising. I'd demanded favor for my boys, and felt I'd been rebuffed.

MARY: You are their mother. It's perfectly natural.

SALOME: But see how He's answered my prayers. And not at all the way I expected. He entrusted you, John, with the care of His mother.

JOHN: Yes, I see.

SALOME: And James. How brave he was to give his witness before Agrippa and all those others.

MARY: God has used your son mightily. And John—your other son—he's been such a blessing to me!

JOHN: And you to me . . . Mother.

SALOME: Yes . . . "Mother" . . .

JOHN: Mother, I didn't mean . . .

SALOME: John, I want you to know I'm so proud of you. I think your father would be just as proud if he were still with us.

JOHN: I'm very proud of my brother.

SALOME: So am I. I only regret I never took the chance to tell him.

MARY: I'm sure he knows, Salome. He knows now.

SALOME: Yes, he knows now. *(Rises from chair)* Now, I must go out there and thank them for coming.

JOHN: Are you sure, Mother?

SALOME: Yes, my son, I am sure. Besides, we must also pray for Peter. *(*MARY *and* JOHN *go on either side of her.)* Tell me, Mary, have you been able to get him to watch that temper of his? It wasn't for nothing Jesus called my boys "Sons of Thunder."

MARY: Oh, he has his moments. I think we all do.

(They begin to move toward SL until JOHN *stops.)*

JOHN: Do either of you know how blessed I am to have two wonderful mothers?

MARY: Oh, John!

SALOME: Let us go. They need us.

(They exit SL.)